Need to Know

Family Break-up

Keeley Bishop
Penny Tripp

Heinemann
LIBRARY

www.heinemann.co.uk/library

Visit our website to find out more information about **Heinemann Library** books.

To order:

☎ Phone 44 (0) 1865 888066

📄 Send a fax to 44 (0) 1865 314091

🖥 Visit the Heinemann Bookshop at www.heinemann.co.uk/library to browse our catalogue and order online.

Produced by Roger Coote Publishing
Gissing's Farm, Fressingfield, Suffolk IP21 5SH, UK

First published in Great Britain by Heinemann Library, Halley Court, Jordan Hill, Oxford OX2 8EJ, part of Harcourt Education.
Heinemann is a registered trademark of Harcourt Education Ltd.

Editorial: Penny Tripp
Design: Jamie Asher
Picture Research: Sally Smith
Production: Viv Hichens

Originated by Ambassador Litho Ltd
Printed and bound in China by South China Printing Company

ISBN 0 431 09810 7
07 06 05 04 03
10 9 8 7 6 5 4 3 2 1

British Library Cataloguing in Publication Data
Bishop, Keeley
Family break-up. - (Need to know)
1.Divorce - Juvenile literature 2. Children of divorced parents - Juvenile literature 3. Teenagers - Family relationships - Juvenile literature
I.Title II.Tripp, Penny
306.8'9

Acknowledgements
The Publishers would like to thank the following for permission to reproduce photographs: AKG London p. 10-11 (Erich Lessing); Collections pp. 1 top (Kim Naylor), 7 top (Kim Naylor), 33 (Graeme Peacock), 38 (Nigel Hawkins), 42 (Liz Stares); Corbis pp. 5 (Ariel Skelley), 19 (SIE Productions), 48 (Julian Hirshowitz); Format pp. 23 (Paula Solloway), 34 (Michael Ann Mullen), 39 (Ulrike Press), 50-51 (Paula Solloway); ImageState *front cover (foreground);* John Birdsall Photography pp. 7 bottom, 8, 9, 31; Mary Evans Picture Library p. 6; Network Photographers pp. 25 (Jenny Matthews), 35 (Jenny Matthews); Photofusion pp. 1 bottom (Ute Klaphake), 17 (Ute Klaphake), 21 (Christa Stadtler), 27 (Christa Stadtler), 28 (Ute Klaphake), 29 (Ute Klaphake), 37 (Ute Klaphake), 41 (Paul Baldesare); Popperfoto p. 13; Rex Features pp. 14-15 (Bill Ray/Timepix), 45, *front cover (background)* (Amanda Knapp); Sally and Richard Greenhill pp. 20, 43; Science Photo Library p. 46-47 (Will and Deni McIntyre); Skjold Photographs p. 36.

Every effort has been made to contact copyright holders of any material reproduced in this book. Any omissions will be rectified in subsequent printings if notice is given to the publishers.

Any words appearing in the text in bold, **like this**, are explained in the Glossary.

Contents

Family break-up

Twenty-first-century families come in all sorts of shapes and sizes. Gone are the days when 'family' automatically meant a pair of married parents and their children.

A hundred years ago, family break-up was much less common than it is now. When people got married, they expected to stay married to the same person until one or other of them died. They had children who lived with them until the children found husbands and wives of their own.

People still get married, have children and live together happily ever after, but the fact is that a lot of them do not. Nearly half of all US and Australian marriages end in **divorce**, and so do many British marriages. Today's children are much more likely than their grandparents to experience the break-up of their family – around one in four of them will spend at least part of their childhood with only one parent.

The family you live with right now might be your mother and father plus you and some brothers and sisters. Another typical modern family could be a mother and father and just a single child. One friend might live with her mother and her mother's new **partner** and their children – another might live with his father and brothers and sisters.

You may also know people living with a grandparent or an aunt or an older cousin who looks after them.

Confusing? You bet

Things can get still more confusing. Even families that seem happy and settled can fall apart. A family member may die or leave, or parents separate because they can no longer live together. Whatever the reasons behind family break-up, its impact on everyone involved can be enormous.

For some people, it is only slightly less painful than dealing with death. They can experience the same kind of feelings when their family breaks up as they do when someone close to them dies – disbelief, anger, sadness. For others, it may be easier.

This book looks at the reasons why families break up and what happens when they do.

What is a family?

There have been families as long as there have been people. They are different all over the world, but until as recently as a hundred years ago, most children in **Westernized societies** – in the UK, USA, Europe and Australia for example – lived with their father and mother. They might well have had many brothers and sisters – in 1900 the average number of children in a British family was seven. This kind of **nuclear family** is much less common now – and not just because adult couples tend to have fewer children.

A twenty-first-century family can be said to exist when a child lives with at least one parental figure. Children today might live with two or more adults, or just one. A pair of adults in a family group might be married to each other, or they might not. They might belong to the same sex, or be one male and one female. One of the adults might be the child's **biological parent** – their mother or father – or both of them might be. Some children live in families parented by adults who are not related to them in any way, because they are **adopted** or **fostered**. Others live with members of their **extended family** – someone like their grandparents, or an aunt or older cousin. In some countries – Russia, China and in southern Asia, for example – most family units are still large. Grandparents, aunts, uncles and older children continue to live together.

Large, close-knit families bound together by marriage – like this American family a hundred years ago – are less common today.

6

An alternative lifestyle

In other places, all over the world, families join together to live and work in **communes**. Different communes have different reasons for existing. Some people live in them because they think they offer a better way of sharing responsibilities – including caring for children – than more traditional family units. Others do so because they want to live and work with people who have the same goals in life. Many communes are based on shared religious ideas, while some focus more on what it means to live together and support other people as members of a group.

Children brought up in such groups may think of themselves as having many parents, rather than just two biological parents. They have close family-type relationships with many people who are not related to them.

❝A family is somewhere you live and are loved and cared for.❞

(Rupinder, aged 14)

Today's parents are less likely to be married for life than their grandparents were.

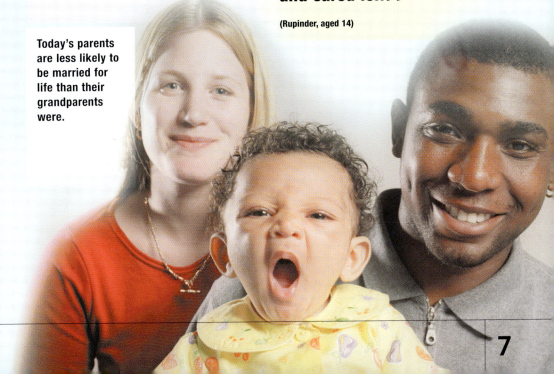

7

What is family break-up?

Some family break-ups happen after a long period of unhappiness. Others are sudden. All are difficult to handle, and everyone experiences them in different ways.

Separation and divorce

Parents who decide to part may do so for one reason or for many. They may no longer share the same interests, or feel the same way about each other, as they once did. Disagreements may have turned into constant arguments. One might find the other's behaviour impossible, or have met someone else they want to live with.

When an adult leaves after a long period of unhappiness and anger, those remaining may feel relieved that they have gone. If the break-up is sudden, they are more likely to be angry, confused and bewildered.

Children often feel that their parents' break-up is somehow their fault. They may understand very little about what has happened, and the remaining adult may be so upset or angry that they cannot easily talk about it with them.

Death or disappearance of a family member

Some families are broken up by death. Some deaths happen suddenly, while others are expected. Someone dying after a long illness may leave the rest of the family feeling sad, but relieved they are now out of pain. The sudden death of a family member can lead to feelings of grief, anger or sadness that can be very difficult to express.

Sometimes, people simply go missing. There may have been an argument, or the person who left may have felt that they just could not continue living as part of the family any more. They may have felt unloved, or as if they were to blame for everything bad that happened.

Some families stay together forever, but others may not.

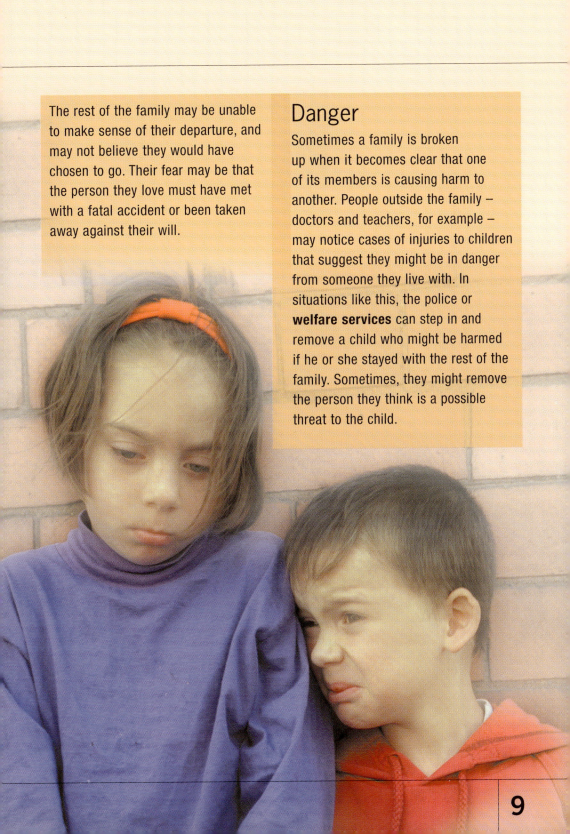

The rest of the family may be unable to make sense of their departure, and may not believe they would have chosen to go. Their fear may be that the person they love must have met with a fatal accident or been taken away against their will.

Danger

Sometimes a family is broken up when it becomes clear that one of its members is causing harm to another. People outside the family – doctors and teachers, for example – may notice cases of injuries to children that suggest they might be in danger from someone they live with. In situations like this, the police or **welfare services** can step in and remove a child who might be harmed if he or she stayed with the rest of the family. Sometimes, they might remove the person they think is a possible threat to the child.

The first families

Why did family groups first appear?

There have been people on Earth for almost two million years. Our species has survived where others have not, despite the fact that in some ways it seems badly equipped. Many animals fend for themselves almost from the moment of birth, but our young need care for many years if they are to make it into healthy adulthood. They rely heavily on their parents' **nurturing** instinct – a strong in-built desire to look after their offspring – and survival skills. Without these they die, and so does the species.

Early humans lived wherever they could find shelter, food and water. Their world was full of powerful predators. Even a relatively strong grown-up could be killed by a mammoth or savaged by a sabre-toothed cat. Our ancestors had no food unless they caught it, killed it, picked it off a plant or dug it up.

Males, females and their young probably banded together with other small family groups because that way they were more powerful – and therefore more likely to survive – than they were by themselves. A single **nuclear family** would have had no chance if one of its adults became sick, was injured or died.

Families through time

Slowly, over tens of thousands of years, living conditions changed. Even so, family groups formed the basis of societies all over the world. Deep-rooted instinctive, emotional and social ties kept them together.

In some cultures, it was the parents of a nuclear family who had primary responsibility for

Ancient Egyptian paintings and sculptures often show husbands and wives with their arms around each other.

the welfare of their own children. Others organized themselves into societies based on **communes**, where children were looked after by the group as a whole rather than by their **biological parents**. If a parent left the group for any reason, children still had others they could depend on until they could look after themselves.

By 5000 years ago, the Ancient Egyptians had written laws about what a family was – and penalties for those who broke them. People who ignored or did not conform to the rules laid down by their religions – or who just acted differently from those around them – had a price to pay.

Families in Ancient Egypt
• A girl was usually married by the time she was 14. Her husband was probably aged around 20.
• There was no official marriage ceremony. People were 'married' when they started living together, and '**divorced**' when they split up.
• Some couples' marriages were arranged for them by their parents – especially if both families were rich and powerful, and wanted to become even more so – but others married because they loved each other.
• Important men often had many wives, and some kings had hundreds.
• The chief wife was her husband's equal. She ran the house, owned all the household goods, and had her own servants.

Family break-up in history

A hundred years ago a typical family in the USA, Europe or Australia was usually made up of a married couple and their children. Men were generally the people responsible for making decisions in public life – in business and politics, for example. They usually only got married when they had enough money to support a wife and children. They might inherit this money when their parents died or, more often, have to work for it. Women rarely worked outside the home. Their job was to run the household – using the money their husband supplied – and bring up the children.

Marriage was considered to be the foundation for a proper family life, and anybody who had a sexual relationship outside marriage was frowned upon. Women who became pregnant without a husband were often sent away from home until their babies were born, and were thought to have brought shame on their families. Their **illegitimate** children had no father's name on their birth certificate, and few legal rights.

Marriage may have been the only way anybody could have a 'proper' sexual relationship and **legitimate** children a hundred years ago, but that did not mean all marriages were happy. An unhappy marriages could be brought to a legal end by **divorce**. This process was difficult and involved having to prove that one partner – usually the wife – had been guilty of unacceptable behaviour.

A woman's adultery – having a sexual relationship outside her marriage – was sufficient reason for a husband to divorce her, but she could not divorce him if he did the same thing! A divorced woman's children became her ex-husband's property, and he could stop her from ever seeing them. Adulterers and **divorcees**, especially women, were thought to be a bad influence on children and incapable of caring for them properly. Getting married for a second time, unless a previous husband or wife had died, was almost unheard of.

During the 20th century, huge numbers of men left home – sometimes for years on end – to fight for their countries during two world wars. Families broke up while they were away, sometimes forever. Many women filled the jobs the men left empty and, instead of depending on their husbands for financial

support, earned their own money for the first time. Those whose husbands were killed brought up their children as best they could.

Even in the 1950s, society and its laws still decreed that marriage was for ever, and that there was no place for sex – or children – outside it. Childcare experts said that parents who separated or divorced would damage their children, and people believed them.

During World War II, women who had never worked outside their homes took on jobs previously done only by men.

Family break-up since 1960

Families in the middle of the 20th century had fewer children than before, partly because they no longer had to have lots to make sure that one or two survived until adulthood. Some of the childhood illnesses that used to kill children in their thousands could now be cured, and others prevented altogether. People were generally eating better food, had access to better medical care and were living longer lives. More and more women were working outside the home, and some were even earning enough to be financially independent. They no longer had to rely on finding a suitable husband to look after them, because they could look after themselves.

Marriage and children, though, still went hand-in-hand. Many young people were pressurized into marriage because their relationship had led to an unplanned pregnancy.

The 1960s

Boys and girls in their late teens in the 1960s had more options than to stay at home and wait to get married in order to be independent of their parents. They could find jobs and earn a living, or go away to college and continue their education. It became more common for young people to move away from home before they were married. They no longer had to rely on their parents for money.

By the late 1960s, people could have sexual relationships without having children, because the **contraceptive** pill was widely available – even to unmarried women. It was gradually becoming more acceptable for men and women to live together without being married, and getting married was something that people could now choose to do rather than have to. They also wanted the same freedom to get **divorced** if a marriage did not work out.

The 1970s onwards

Since the 1970s, fewer people have chosen to marry. There are twice as many single-parent families today as there were then. Some are that way because parents have divorced, others because people have chosen to bring up their children without being married. By 1998, around one in four US-based children lived with a single parent – 84% of them with their mothers – and in the UK, 8% of families with children were headed by an unmarried couple living together.

Young people in the 1960s not only started to dress differently from their parents, but to think differently too. Many of the old rules were changing.

Family change in the USA

	1970	2000
Family groups with children	30 million	37 million
Single-mother families	3 million (12% of all families)	10 million (26% of all families)
Single-father families	393,000 (1% of all families)	2 million (5% of all families)

(Source: US Census Bureau, 2001. www.census.gov)

Current trends

So many families have experienced break-up of some kind that it is no longer considered unusual. Statistics show that all the industrialized nations are experiencing similar trends – family units are breaking up and becoming smaller, and fewer children are being born.

Marriage is becoming less popular, and almost half end in **divorce**. Every day in the UK, 650 children see their parents separate or divorce. In Australia, around a quarter of the country's 4.6 million under-18s live with only one of their **biological parents**.

Families today

Single-parent families are twice as common as they were in the 1970s. At one time, the children of divorcing parents were automatically thought to be better off living with their mothers, with their fathers giving financial support and having **contact** or visiting rights. More fathers are now successfully arguing that they are just as capable of bringing children up on their own as mothers are. Divorced mothers and fathers are increasingly being encouraged to share responsibility for the children they brought into the world.

Being divorced does not now make it impossible to marry again, or to set up home with someone else. Families formed when this happens – **step-families** – are becoming more common: two-and-a-half million children in the UK live with people to whom they are not related by birth. **Blended families** are formed when a parent goes on to have children with a new **partner**, who may also have children from a previous relationship.

Some children are born to parents who cannot take responsibility for them. Young mothers and fathers who are still at school, for example, may want a better life for their child than they feel they can give. Other parents may suffer from a physical or mental illness that makes it very hard for them to look after a child. In this kind of situation, a child can be **adopted** or **fostered** by another family. The law is changing in some countries to allow adoption by unmarried couples who can show that they can offer a child a stable home and meet its needs.

"I live with my mum during the week, and with my grandparents at weekends. I sometimes see my dad on Sundays."

(Michael, aged 14)

Many children today live with their mother for part of the week, and their father for the rest of the week.

Reasons why families break up

Family break-up can happen after a long period of unhappiness, or very suddenly. A family may split apart after years of arguments and violent disagreements, in spite of many attempts to keep it whole. Parents may look for outside help either separately or together – from **counsellors** or members of their church, for example – before making a final decision to part. Another family might experience the sudden – and permanent – departure of one of its members. A parent or child could die, for instance, or might suddenly leave because they feel they can no longer stay.

Drifting apart

Shared interests, ideas and values are the basis for many relationships but interests and ideas can change, or differences of opinion become more important than they once were. A couple might gradually realize that they no longer have anything in common, and that there does not seem to be any point in staying together.

Wanting to be with someone else

Even people who think they are happy together can – slowly or in an instant – fall in love with someone else. They cannot imagine living without them, even though they know that leaving their present **partner** will be difficult and painful. Falling in love is not something that people choose to do – many say that 'it just happened' – but it is a powerful feeling and hard to ignore.

Wanting to go in different directions

When a couple get together, they tend to agree on the direction their lives will take. They know what kind of work they want to do, how they will spend their free time, what their long-term ambitions are. Their plans cannot take into account something they haven't even thought of – like one partner's realization that they cannot get what they really want if they stay with their partner.

Failure to agree

Many couples argue about money, but it is not the only thing they disagree about. When they find little common ground on anything, and arguments arise all the time without being settled, life becomes so difficult that parting may be the only option. Other families may accept that their arguments are a normal part of family life, and remain strong and settled in spite of them.

Abuse

Most people today agree that it is never acceptable to use physical violence against a child, or for one adult to use violence against another. Violence within a family is often hidden, and can sometimes go on for a long time without anyone outside knowing about it. So can sexual **abuse** of one family member by another. People who misuse alcohol or other drugs can become aggressive and violent towards other family members, or neglect their parental responsibilities. Sometimes breaking up a family is the only way to keep non-abusing family members safe and well.

Some parents argue all the time and still have a strong relationship, but others become frustrated and angry if they feel they cannot agree on anything.

The normal family

'Normal' families in 21st-century industrialized societies reflect the fact that family break-up is far more common than it was 50 years ago. In the USA alone, 20 million children live with just one parent. Families arrange themselves in so many different ways after break-up that it is hard to know now what 'normal' is.

When couples separate, they sometimes feel a lot of bitterness and anger towards their ex-**partner** and find it hard to agree on who their children should live with. In some situations it is obvious where they will be better off, in others less so. Children's own views are more often listened to than they used to be.

Parents who no longer live with their children are usually encouraged to see them regularly – they do not stop being a parent when they **divorce** – unless they are thought to be a danger to the child.

Living with mother

Around 84% of children live with their mother after their parents split, sometimes in the same family home as before, sometimes in a new one. Some – over four million of them in the USA – live with their mother in their grandparents' house. Many see their fathers regularly, but some do not.

Living with father

It is becoming more common for children to live with their father after a separation. For many years it was thought that fathers could not look after their children properly, but this is changing as men become more involved in parenting and more women take on demanding full-time jobs.

Step-families

When a child's mother or father divorce to form a relationship with someone new, their new partner may have children of their own. If they then marry, the two families join together and the children find themselves living with step-brothers and sisters.

Joint custody

Some children live with their mothers for some of the time, and with their fathers for the rest. Their parents share responsibility for their welfare just as they did before they broke up.

Flexible arrangements

When parents divorce, they have to decide where their children will live and who will look after them. These arrangements do not have to stay the same forever, and can be changed later as long as everyone involved agrees.

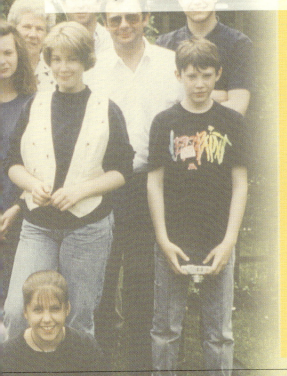

Leonie

Leonie's mum formed another relationship with a man who was also divorced. He had two children of his own who lived with their mother, but who stayed with their dad every other weekend. In the beginning, this was on the same weekends that Leonie was away seeing her dad.

'I used to get really cross at first,' says Leonie. 'Ian and Lucy came and stayed in my room, and got to do fun things with their dad and my mum. My room was always a mess, and I know they went through my things. I hated it. I couldn't believe my mum would let them do this.'

Leonie's mum and dad changed their weekends around, and relationships improved. Leonie now joins in the family's activities, and no longer feels she is missing out.

Changes

Family is the most important and powerful thing in the lives of most children. If one of their parents dies, or their mother and father split up, or someone they care about leaves their family, children may think that the love and stability they knew have gone forever. Although it can feel like that at first, most children eventually get used to the kind of changes a family break-up brings. If family life has meant a lot of arguments and unhappiness, a break-up can be a relief and things may seem a lot better afterwards.

Frequently-asked questions

Faced with huge changes, children and young people ask questions. Some are very difficult to answer, and parents have to deal with them while they cope with their own fears about what the future holds.

Who will be responsible for me?

Children sometimes fear that a parent leaving means that they are going to end up completely on their own. They may even be afraid that the other parent will disappear, too.

Where will I live? Do I have any choice?

If the parent leaving is the one they feel closest to, children may be deeply troubled at the thought of not going with them. They may fear having to choose between two people they love. When they associate a parent with violence or **abuse**, they may be afraid that they will be forced to stay with them or have to see them even if they don't want to.

What will I say to my friends?

Children often think that their own family is the only one that has ever been through a break-up. They may not realize that they know lots of other people it has happened to.

They may worry that their friends will see them and their family as odd, or embarrassing. If the break-up means a move out of the area, they may be afraid that they will never see their friends again.

Young people whose lives are changing can find it helpful to talk to friends. Girls often find this easier than boys.

Changes

Is it my fault?

Although parents say their children are never to blame for family break-up, children do not always see it that way. They remember times when they made a parent angry, or when they seemed to be the reason for a disagreement. They think that if only they had been good, this would not be happening. But families do not break up because children have been naughty.

What will happen to my pets?

Worrying that one change will automatically lead to others, children may feel that they are going to lose everything that is important to them.

Will we be poor?

Children may worry about whether they can still have treats, outings and birthday presents, especially if the parent they will be living with does not work outside the home.

Can I make contact with Mum or Dad when I want?

Children who are close to a parent who is leaving want to know if they can stay in touch. Telephone calls, emails, letters, visits and outings can all help, and they need to know whether they can make the first move rather than just wait. On the other hand, a child who has had bad experiences with the parent who is leaving needs reassurance that they will not be forced to see them if they do not want to.

Will we live as a family again?

A child who loves both their parents and cannot really understand why they are breaking up may hope for a long time that they will get back together again.

Email can be a good way of sharing news with family members who live somewhere else.

Making changes

Making changes can be hard when people do not agree on what should happen next. Most families who break up work things out by themselves, maybe with the help of friends and relations and other advisors. Others find it more difficult. Professional **mediators** – people who are trained to help others reach agreement – can work with quarrelling parents to sort out arrangements about who lives where, how the bills are going to be paid, and ways of keeping in contact with each other.

If families cannot agree, a **judge** or **magistrate** may have to decide for them, and make a **court order** that tells them what they can and cannot do. Before they do this, they find out what both parents and children want.

Common reactions

Most young people who have experienced a separation from one or both of their parents clearly remember the moment they realized what was happening. How they react depends on the reasons for the separation, the kind of atmosphere surrounding it – fear, sadness, relief or hostility – and how old they are. Although a family break-up may feel frightening and difficult at first, most people find that things get easier over time.

Birth to two years old

Children under two years old are highly dependent on their parents. They are especially close to the person who they are with the most. These children do not understand what is happening to their family, but they are acutely aware of the stress and anxiety of those around them. If a person who usually looks after them is away for any length of time, they miss them and fret for them.

Two to five years old

Separation can be a major shock to children in this age group. Anger, sadness and anxiety are common reactions, and children as young as this can even show signs of depression. They may show their distress by behaving as they did when they were younger, doing things they seemed to have grown out of – like bedwetting, having nightmares and thumb-sucking. Some start using 'baby-talk' again. Pre-school children make sense of their world in very different ways from older children, and may make up stories to explain things they do not understand.

Six to eight years old

It is the children in this age group who seem to have the hardest time coping with family break-up. They commonly experience great sadness, and feelings of being unlovable. They often feel that the departing parent is rejecting them. They may find it hard to concentrate at school, and start behaving in ways that alert friends, teachers and parents to the fact that they are feeling bad. They cannot explain how they feel in words. They want their family back how it was, and often do and say things to try and make this happen.

Common reactions

Nine to twelve years old

At this age, most children have friends and interests outside their family. Although their family is still very important to them, it is no longer their only world. They feel shock and sadness when their family breaks up, and these feelings often turn to anger against the parent who leaves. Although they understand more about what is happening than younger children do, they can still feel powerless, helpless and rejected. They worry about the future and what will happen to them. Their school work often suffers. Unlike younger children, however, they can put their feelings into words and accept help and reassurance from those around them.

Adolescents

Young people over the age of 12 are usually more independent of their families, and more influenced than younger children by reactions from their friends. They tend to distance themselves from both parents while they try to understand their feelings. They worry about what the break-up will mean for their future – will they be able to stay at the same school? Go to college? Keep their current friends? If they have been aware for a long time that relationships within the family were difficult, they may feel relief that the stress is over.

Feeling lonely and sad is a very common reaction to family break-up.

Long-term reactions

Ten years on from family break-up, young people report many mixed feelings about what happened. How they manage to cope with it seems in all cases to be directly related to the way their behave. An atmosphere of parental co-operation rather than conflict means that children can adjust to the changes in their own way and their own time. Constant parental fighting leaves children with long-term feelings of sadness and insecurity, and they find it hard to feel good about themselves.

"After the divorce my mum started acting like she was my best friend. She even wanted to talk about this guy she fancied, and was always pinching my make-up and clothes. I got really fed up about this. My mates were all talking about her and I told her to back off. In the end though I just had to realize it was just a phase she was going through."

(Mia, aged 16, from *Torn in Two* by Matthew Whyman, 1997)

Social and welfare services

Sometimes family break-ups involve more people than those who are directly concerned. Neighbours, teachers or health workers who deal regularly with family members may become worried about their health, or their safety, or how they are behaving. In some cases they may report their concerns to the police – or others who are legally responsible for the welfare of people in the community – who may then step in.

Some of these people work for government-funded social and **welfare services**. Others are employed by locally based public authorities to make sure that individuals and families – especially children – get help when they need it.

Why do welfare services get involved?

Parents who are physically or mentally ill may not be able to look after their children properly. Others may have drug-use or alcohol habits that affect how they behave. Some may have violent tempers that they cannot control. When they are angry, they may lash out at people close to them and hurt them. Some adults – called **paedophiles** – are sexually attracted to children rather than people their own age, and try to involve children in illegal sexual relationships.

In situations like these, where children are neglected or hurt, the welfare services can call on the power of the law to remove them from the family to protect them and keep them safe.

How do welfare services get involved?

Those who come into contact with children – teachers and health workers, for example – are trained to recognize the signs of neglect or **abuse**. If they suspect that a child is not being properly looked after, they may report their concerns to the welfare services or police, and explain why they are worried. Sometimes neighbours or friends raise the alarm.

Outsiders sometimes step in to help sort out family difficulties. This kind of help is not always easy to accept.

31

Social and welfare services

There are special police units whose job it is to help families in difficulties. They protect children and other people at risk, often working closely with welfare services. They may suggest classes or **counselling** sessions for parents who find it hard to support their children, but who want to stay together as a family. They have the power to remove a family member who is in danger, or who is a threat to others. In situations where children are thought to be in immediate or serious danger, they can be removed from their family. This can only happen after a proper investigation, and may involve presenting a **judge** with evidence in **court**.

Removing children from their families is a last resort. It is done when they are thought to be in real danger – from neglect or harm – if they remain. If their own family environment is not safe, children then need to be found a new home. There may be family friends or relations who can offer them one. If not, they may be found one with people who will **foster** them for a while, or **adopt** them permanently.

Fostering

Foster families are people willing to care for children who are not their own, until the children can go back to their own homes or be found a permanent one elsewhere. Anyone wanting to be a foster parent is checked carefully by the welfare services to make sure that they can offer children a safe and secure place to live. In return, they get financial support from the welfare services who place children with them.

Some foster parents have children of their own, but others do not. Children are often placed with foster parents who live close by, so that they can see other members of their own family and their friends, and keep going to the same school. Some foster children may stay only until they can go back to their own families, or until they move to a family that wants to adopt them.

Adoption

Children who cannot live with their own family for some reason may be adopted, and become a permanent and legal part of a new family. They may be adopted because their own parents have died, perhaps by someone belonging to their **extended family**. Children becoming part of a **step-family** are sometimes adopted by their step-father or step-mother. Other children may be adopted by individuals or couples completely unrelated to them – people who have said they want to bring them up as their own, and shown that they can offer the right kind of home.

After family break-up

Once a family has broken up, it is unlikely to come back together again in the same shape. The difficulties and differences that cause parents to part do not vanish just because they have separated or have a piece of paper that tells them they are **divorced**. The children of separated parents may at least see their **absent parent** sometimes, but it can take a long time for a family to get used to living without a parent who has died.

The year after break-up in particular sees everyone making practical and emotional adjustments to a new way of life. It can be a confusing and unsettling time, but it does not last forever.

Living with one parent and visiting the other

Children used to living with two parents can find it hard to adjust to seeing one of them all the time, and the other only occasionally. Sometimes formal arrangements are laid down – in a divorce agreement, for example – about who can see each other. There may be rules about how often this can happen, where visiting takes place, and how long each visit can last. Children can feel torn between their parents, especially if there has been disagreement over who they are to live with.

It takes time to get used to moving to a new school, and to spending more time with one parent than another.

Everybody reacts to family break-up in their own way.

Having two homes

Children may have two homes – one they live in most of the time, and another where they visit the parent who has left. Some find this exciting and different, others find it confusing. All may find leaving one of their homes to go to the other hard to cope with.

Changing schools

Older children may find a move and a change of school especially difficult, as their lives outside the family are important to them. School means stability and friendships, and moving to a new one may leave them feeling unsettled and lost.

Not seeing one parent

Children may be prevented from seeing a parent because they are thought by the **welfare services** to be at risk if they do. Their feelings in this situation may be complex – even if a parent has been neglectful, or has harmed someone in the family, they may still be loved by their children. On the other hand, everybody may be glad the parent is no longer involved with the family, but still find it hard to adjust to their absence.

New families

Step-families

Single parents may re-marry or form new long-term relationships that bring children into **step-families**. The new partner becomes a step-parent to the children, and their children become step-brothers and step-sisters.

Life in a step-family can be very difficult to begin with. Children tend to compare their new step-parent with their 'real' parent. They may have to share a home with people they do not know well. They also have to share their parent – with the parent's new partner, and with other children. There may be new family rules to get used to. As the initial strangeness wears off and relationships form, things usually get better.

Foster homes

Children and young people removed from their families by outside agencies – like the **welfare services** – often do not understand why they have to leave. They may find themselves separated from their brothers and sisters as well as their parents, and living with a **foster** family they do not know. It might be just for a few weeks – while the parent who normally cares for them is in hospital, for example – or for a longer time. They are often angry and confused. They think that people are not listening to them, and are not interested in what they want. Their parents may be angry and resentful that the family has been broken up, but unable or unwilling to make the changes that would mean it could come together again.

Adoptive homes

Children may be **adopted** by their step-parents, or by people previously unknown to them who can offer the kind of stable, settled home their own parents cannot provide. Fitting into any new family can be hard at first, especially if a child has already experienced a lot of changes in his or her family life. Sometimes social or welfare workers may visit to help sort out any difficulties.

Some people who have been adopted might know very little about their **biological parents**. Adoptive parents may not always know very much about them either. Some children may want to know about them, and others do not. Some want to find out about them when they are grown up, or when they have children of their own, and there are ways of helping them do this.

❝At first it was horrible. I had to live with people I didn't know – and in their house. They had rules that I didn't know about, but everyone else did.❞

(Brad, aged 13)

37

Keeping in touch

Family break-up can mean that one household becomes two, and children see less of the parent they no longer live with. The official name given to the times when children see their **absent parent** is '**contact**' or '**visitation**'.

Many young people say that regular contact with both parents helped them deal with the emotional upheaval surrounding family break-up. Continued contact helps them to understand that a parent still loves them even if they live somewhere else.

Ways of keeping in touch

Separated families keep in touch in all sorts of ways. It might be through weekly visits, or going to stay every weekend or once a month. Some people keep in touch through phone calls, emails and letters. Some families use web pages and web cams, while others regularly exchange videos and photographs.

Why does contact help?

Children who do not have regular contact with one of their parents can grow up with an unrealistic view of what that parent is really like. They might come to imagine them as all good, or all bad. Few parents really fall into these two categories, and a child in regular contact with both its parents will be able to see the true picture.

Continuing contact with an absent parent helps children feel part of a loving family, even if all the members of it do not live together. Staying in touch means that

family members can continue
to share experiences and keep each
other up-to-date with what is
happening to them. It is especially
important if brothers or sisters
– or maybe even grandparents
or other family members – are now
living with the absent parent.

Saying 'goodbye' at the end of
a visit can be difficult, but
usually gets easier over time.

39

When contact is difficult

When parents separate or **divorce**, they may find it hard to agree on when, where and how children and the absent parent are to see each other. Difficulties in arranging contact times usually have more to do with the parents' relationship with each other than anything children do. Even when an agreement has been reached, some parents find it hard to stick to it. One parent may feel so angry with the other that they cannot encourage and support their child's relationship with them. Another may be so upset by what has happened that they cannot bear their children to go anywhere near their former partner. Some children find themselves passing messages between their parents because the adults find it so hard to talk directly. This changes over time, but is common to begin with.

Kids-in-the-middle

In this kind of situation, children may hear one parent say all sorts of critical things about (or to) the other – almost as if they think the child is deaf, or not there. 'Of course, she's always late!' and 'You'd rather go out with your friends than see the children anyway' might be some of them. Other comments may be directly addressed to the children – 'Your father was never any good at keeping his promises!', for example. This kind of talk can often sound to children as if one parent is trying to turn them against the other. Sometimes this is true, but more often it is an expression of how hurt and angry the parent feels.

Sometimes children feel as if one parent is trying to get them to spy on the other, and be unwilling to say anything about what they do when they are with them for fear of causing an argument or upsetting anybody. Children can end up feeling like ping-pong balls bouncing between separated parents. There may be nothing they can do to keep them both happy at this stage, but many children try.

No contact

There may be times when it is impossible for children to see one of their parents – if they are at risk of violence or other harm, for example, or if either parent finds it too difficult. As the child gets older, though, it may become possible again.

"Before contact was sorted, I spent my weekends on the train travelling between my parents 'cos I didn't want to upset anyone."

(Jack, aged 15)

Religious views

It is becoming more common for people to have children without being married, but most of the world's major religions think that marriage is the best way of making sure that children are born into stable and long-lasting families. Within every religious community, however, there are some who believe that parental separation and **divorce** are always wrong, and others who think that it depends on individual circumstances.

In most countries, a legal marriage can be ended by divorce if certain conditions are met. These vary from place to place. Religious marriages can usually be ended, too, but those who belong to some religious communities can find themselves rejected – even by their families – if they divorce.

Christians

Customs vary from country to country, and between the different Christian churches. For example, legally divorced members of the Church of England were unable to re-marry in church for many years, while those who belonged to the Church of Scotland could. Now ministers look at individual cases before making a decision. In the USA, some ultra-strict churches expel **divorcees** who marry for a second time. A Roman Catholic marriage can only be dissolved under certain rare conditions. The Greek Orthodox Church disapproves of divorce, but does not forbid it.

Although more and more couples are choosing not to marry, most religions still believe that marriage is the best way of ensuring that children are properly cared for. But will a marriage last? Nearly half of them now end in divorce.

Muslims

Customs and ideas vary between one branch of Islam and another, and from country to country. There are strict rules about how property should be divided up, and children looked after. Divorcees are not prevented from marrying again, but in some cultures women who do so are frowned upon.

Jews

Within each branch of Judaism – as in all religions – there are ultra-strict and more liberal groups. All recognize divorce, and there is no bar on remarriage.

Hindus

Marriage is an unbreakable holy bond for Hindus, rather than a legal contract as it is for Muslims and Jews. Most communities recognize legal divorce, but some find it hard to believe that a divorced woman – or even a woman whose husband has died – could even think of marrying again.

Sikhs

Like Hindus, Sikhs see marriage as a holy bond but recognize divorces granted in accordance with the law of the land.

Ethical questions

Ethics are the moral values on which nearly all civilizations, societies and communities are based. They provide people with answers to questions like 'What is right?', 'What is wrong?', 'What is good?' and 'What is bad?' It is often very difficult to come up with the 'right' answer to this kind of question.

Are two parents always better than one?

Some children are born to mothers and fathers who are committed to raising their offspring together. Some live happily with both their parents, others with one of them. Some parents successfully bring up their children outside a traditional family structure, either by themselves or with a **partner** of the opposite – or their own – sex.

A two-parent family may not automatically be a good thing. If one parent beats up the children, for example, or spends money on drugs or gambling rather than food, the family may be better off without that person.

Should families always stay together?

At one time, a family stayed together whatever happened and no matter how miserable its members were. Women and children were the property of their husbands and fathers, and men could treat them as they saw fit. If wives and children were **abused** or neglected, there was often nowhere else for them to go. Two hundred years ago, a woman married at 18 might have given birth to 10 children by the time she was 30, and seen most of them die in infancy. She might not even have reached 30.

Things are very different today, and some people argue that rules and customs should not remain fixed when people's lives have changed so dramatically. Medical advances, reliable **contraception**, better nutrition and better housing have all meant that people are living longer and having fewer children than they used to. Women are no longer expected to spend their whole lives raising children and looking after the home. Some earn far more money than the men they choose to have children with, and some are choosing to have no children at all.

Is there such a thing as a 'proper' family?

Trends in **Westernized societies** worldwide show that families are now much more likely to break up than they were even 20 years ago. They also re-form into different shapes. Today's babies may grow up happily within a number of different family groups, or with a single parent. A hundred years ago, family change might only have happened when a parent died.

Even royal families experience family break-up. The future king of England, HRH The Prince of Wales, is divorced and so is his current partner, Camilla Parker-Bowles. Public opinion in the UK is divided as to whether they should marry, and about whether she should become his queen if they do.

Help during family break-up

A family at risk of breaking up, or one that has broken up already, is going through a very difficult time. People may be feeling guilty, or **depressed**, or frightened – sometimes a mixture of all these emotions and more. They may be very short of money. Some may be homeless, others physically hurt or mentally ill. Some feel that what happens to their family is nobody's business but their own, and are unwilling or unable to ask for help from outside. Others – especially children – often don't know where to get help.

Friends and relations

Young people whose family is breaking up can feel very alone. They may be able to talk to an aunt, uncle or grandparent about what's happening at home, but sometimes worry that they are being disloyal. They might also be afraid that what they say will lead to trouble – for them, or for another family member. Often they find that talking to someone they know and trust helps them feel less lonely and more able to cope.

When people don't agree, an outsider can sometimes help.

47

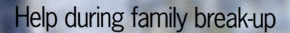

Outside help and advice

Children may find it easier to talk to someone completely outside their family. A trusted teacher or youth worker may be able to offer advice, or put them in touch with someone who can help. Schools and community workers have information about a whole range of support services available to children and families in difficulties. In the USA, schools offer assistance through special support groups, **counsellors** or student-assistance programs.

There are organizations that give emotional and practical support to children and adults dealing with family problems, and contact details for some are listed on pages 52–53.

Counselling and support

Health centres and doctors' surgeries can also put people in touch with someone who will listen to their problems and help them work out what to do next. These counsellors work face-to-face with individual children or parents, with couples, and with families – and sometimes larger groups – depending on what kind of help is needed.

Support groups, sometimes organized and run by local parents or members of religious communities, can also be helpful. Their meetings may be listed in local newspapers or advertised on local radio stations.

Legal help

Some people will never reach agreement without help – perhaps because their situation is complicated, or they are hostile to each other. Many people today have the chance to use the services of a **mediator** – someone who is not on anybody's side, who knows the law, and who can help the couple work together rather than fight things out.

If a couple cannot agree about what should happen to their children, their house or their money, they can each instruct **lawyers** to negotiate for them and speak for them in **court**. A **judge** or **magistrate** listens to both sides of the argument, and comes to a decision for them.

People often turn to grandparents for help during family break-up. Grandchildren often find them easier to talk to than their parents.

Family break-up and the law

Throughout the world, special laws protect the rights of family members. Details vary from one country to another, and one state's family law may be different from another within the same country. Family law covers situations when the police or **welfare services** can step in to protect children and young people thought to be in danger, and can be used to prevent an **abusive** person making contact with other family members. It also covers **divorce**.

Divorce

Divorce is the legal ending of a marriage. In order to get a divorce, a couple has to meet certain conditions and follow a set legal procedure. Conditions and procedures vary. Divorcing couples with children have to show that the children's needs for a

Children's thoughts and feelings are taken into account by the law courts when families break up.

home, financial support, education and **contact** with the parent they will not be living with have all been taken into account. The views of the couple's children are also heard. Some couples agree all the arrangements concerning their children's future, and these are included as part of their divorce.

What if parents cannot agree?

Judges or **magistrates** have the power to make decisions for any parents – not just those who are divorcing – who cannot agree about things to do with their children. These decisions are **court orders**. They may say who the children will live with, and cover arrangements for visiting, phoning and having contact with an **absent parent** or other family members. Judges can also make decisions about how much money one parent should give the other.

If one parent is violent or abusive, a judge can make them leave the family home and not come back, or forbid them from being abusive again. Adults who do not do what the judge orders can be punished.

Information and advice

Contacts in the UK

Telephone helplines

All 0800 numbers are free of charge, and do not show up on a phone bill.

ChildLine
Tel: 0800 1111
www.childline.org.uk
Freephone 24 hours a day, offering free advice to children about a range of family and personal problems.

Children's Legal Centre
Tel: 01206 873820,
www.childrenslegalcentre.com
Although calls have to be paid for, the advice line is open 10 a.m.–12.30 p.m. and 2–4.30 p.m. on weekdays. A free, confidential information service for children and young people – and anyone else wanting legal advice on matters relating to them.

Cruse Bereavement Care
Tel: 020 8332 7227
Help, advice and support if a relative or a friend has died. Lines are open every day, including weekends.

National Youth Advocacy Service
Tel: 0800 616101
Freephone 9 a.m.–9 p.m., Mon–Fri, 2–8 p.m. weekends. Information, advice and someone who can speak for young people needing legal representation.

NSPCC Helpline
Tel: 0800 800500
Freephone 24 hours a day. Counselling, information and advice from the National Society for the Prevention of Cruelty to Children for children at risk of abuse.

Samaritans
Tel: 08457 909090
Freephone 24 hours a day. Advice and support for anyone who is really unhappy or depressed.

Who Cares? Linkline
Tel: 0500 564570
Freephone 3.30–6 p.m., Mon, Wed, Thurs. Advice and support for young people who are or have been in care.

Youth Access
Tel: 020 8772 9900
9.30 a.m.–5.30 p.m. Mon–Fri. Information on where to get help nearby.

Websites

www.carelaw.org.uk
Legal information for young people in care.

www.justask.org.uk
Information, help and advice on legal services.

www.nacab.org.uk
National Association of Citizens Advice Bureaux – advice for everybody about everything.

www.parentlineplus.org.uk
Information and advice on all sorts of family issues. Mainly for parents.

www.thesite.org.uk
Information, help and advice for 15–24 year-olds.

Contacts in the USA

School **counsellors** have information about resources for young people in their local areas.

Contacts in Australia

Child and Youth Health
Tel: 1300 364 100
www.cyh.com.au
Click on Youth Health Link, then Relationships, for information on family break-up and how to deal with it.

Kids Help Line
Tel: 1800 55 1800,
www.kidshelp.com.au
Free helpline for under-18s in difficult situations. Website has lots of useful links to ways of getting help and advice on all sorts of topics.

National Children and Youth Law Centre
www.lawstuff.org.au
Legal rights for under-18s explained, searchable by state and territory.

Reach Out!
www.reachout.com.au
Self-help kit and local contacts.

Disclaimer
All the Internet addresses (URLs) given in this book were valid at the time of going to press. However, due to the dynamic nature of the Internet, some addresses may have changed, or sites may have changed or ceased to exist since publication. While the author and Publisher regret any inconvenience this may cause readers, no responsibility for any such changes can be accepted by either the author or the Publisher.

Further reading

Caught in the Middle: Teenagers Talk about their Parents' Divorce, by Alys Swan-Jackson; Piccadilly Press, 1997

Children Don't Divorce, by Rosemary Stones; Happy Cat Books, 2002

My Family is Splitting Up – A Guide for Young People, Lord Chancellor's Department leaflet (current version available on LCD website – go to **lcd.gov.uk/family/leaflets** and follow the link)

Parent Problems! Children's Views on Life When Parents Split Up, by Bren Neale and Amanda Wade; Young Voice, 2000

The Suitcase Kid, by Jacqueline Wilson; Corgi Yearling, 1993

Torn in Two, by Matthew Whyman; Hodder Children's Books, 1997

Understanding the Law – A Teen Guide to Family Court and Minors' Rights, by Anne Bianchi; Rosen Publishing Group, 1999

Voices of Children of Divorce, by David Royko; St Martin's Press, 2000

Glossary

absent parent
mother or father who does not live with their child

abuse
ill-treatment of someone – by hurting them (physical abuse), forcing them to have sexual contact against their will (sexual abuse), not looking after them properly (neglect), or harming them emotionally (emotional abuse)

adoption
legal process leading to a child being raised by people who are not its biological parents

biological parent
mother or father of a child – that is, the mother who conceived and gave birth to it or the man whose sperm helped create it

blended families
families formed when a parent goes on to have children with a new partner, who may also have children from a previous relationship

commune
alternative to traditional family life, where unrelated people and their families live and work together as a closely-knit group based on shared ideas or goals

contact
child's right or opportunity to stay in touch with an absent parent, or an absent parent's right or opportunity to communicate with its child

contraception
artificial or natural means of preventing pregnancy

counsellors
people trained to give advice and help to others

court
body with the power to hear and make decisions on legal matters

court order
official decision made by a court, with penalties for anyone who does not abide by it

depression
long-lasting mental state that brings with it feelings of deep sadness and worthlessness

divorce
legal ending of a marriage

divorcees
people who are legally divorced

extended family
family members less closely related to someone than their mother, father, brothers
and sisters – for example cousins, uncles, aunts, grandparents

fostered
when a child is housed and cared for temporarily by a family not its own

illegitimate
child born to parents who were not married to each other at the time of its birth

judge
legally qualified public official with the power to preside over legal cases and make decisions (court orders)

lawyer
trained professional who can advise people on legal matters and speak for them in court

legitimate
child born to parents legally married to each other

magistrate
(UK) a non-legally qualified public officer who works in a magistrates' court or family proceedings court to determine the outcome of some family cases

mediators
people who help those involved in disputes to reach agreement

nuclear family
someone's closest relations – for example parents, brothers, sisters

nurturing
encouraging the development of a child

paedophiles
criminal adults who befriend young children because they want illegal sexual relationships with them

partner
either member of a couple in a relationship

step-families
families formed when one or two adults with children form a lasting relationship

visitation
(USA) the child's right or opportunity to stay in touch with an absent parent, or an absent parent's right or opportunity to communicate with his or her child

welfare services
people employed by local or central government to provide help that ensures the well-being of individuals and families in need

Westernized societies
societies that share the kind of customs, laws and values common in the Western – as distinct from the Asian or African – world

Index

Titles in the *Need to Know* series include:

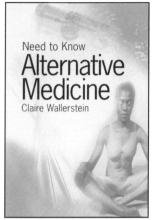

Need to Know
Alternative Medicine
Claire Wallerstein

Hardback   0 431 09808 5

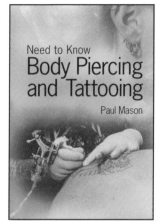

Need to Know
Body Piercing and Tattooing
Paul Mason

Hardback   0 431 09818 2

Need to Know
Depression
Claire Wallerstein

Hardback   0 431 09809 3

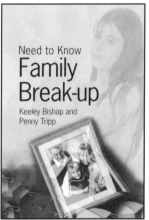

Need to Know
Family Break-up
Keeley Bishop and Penny Tripp

Hardback   0 431 09810 7

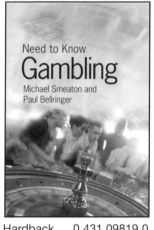

Need to Know
Gambling
Michael Smeaton and Paul Bellringer

Hardback   0 431 09819 0

Need to Know
Painkillers and Tranquillizers
Michael Durham

Hardback   0 431 09811 5

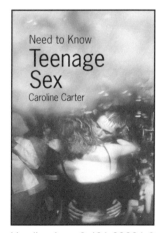

Need to Know
Teenage Sex
Caroline Carter

Hardback   0 431 09821 2

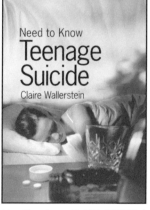

Need to Know
Teenage Suicide
Claire Wallerstein

Hardback   0 431 09820 4

Find out about the other titles in this series on our website www.heinemann.co.uk/library